Proverbs

LIVING A LIFE OF WISDOM

CWR

Ruth Valerio

Published 2005 by CWR, Waverley Abbey House, Waverley Lane, Farnham, Surrey GU9 8EP, UK. Registered Charity No. 294387. Registered Limited Company No. 1990308. Reprinted 2008, 2009, 2010, 2013.

See back of book for list of National Distributors.

Front cover image: Roger Walker
Concept development, editing, design and production by CWR.
Printed in the UK by Page Brothers

ISBN: 978-1-85345-373-1

Contents

Introduction

A popular UK radio programme hosts a lunchtime topical chat show. Each day it takes an item for debate that is current in the news, has one or two 'experts' in to comment on it and then opens the discussion up to the listening public. The issues vary enormously – from teenage pregnancies to tackling poverty in Africa, and from the rights of a person to die how they want to the wearing of burkhas by Muslim women.

What comes over continuously is that none of these issues is simple or has a clear-cut answer. It takes wisdom to know how to deal with these, and other, issues. As Christians we face daily a barrage of questions as to how we can live God's way in this world which, though created by Him, has chosen a different path. In addition, nowhere are Christians promised immunity from the harsh realities of life. It takes wisdom to know how, as followers of Jesus, we can steer a straight course through life's choppy waters.

The good news is that it is precisely this sort of wisdom that we are promised in the book of Proverbs, which was written to help the people of God remain true to Him in a complicated world.[1] For that to happen we need discipline, insight, prudence, knowledge and discernment, and Proverbs promises us that these can be ours if we take care to listen and not forsake the teaching that is found in this book. Studying this book will be refreshing because wisdom is something that we do not tend to talk about much in our culture today. We might talk about being clever or knowledgeable or learned, but not so much about being *wise*. According to Proverbs, wisdom does encompass cleverness, knowledge and learning (see 2:6), but it goes further than that. Rooted as it is in the fear of the Lord, it goes beyond the world of academia and books into our everyday lives. Again and again in Proverbs we will see how immensely practical this idea of wisdom is. It is not some ethereal concept that is of no earthly good, but is concerned with the everyday realities of life.

As you will see throughout this guide, Proverbs reveals its wisdom through a series of contrasts. On the one hand there is the invitation and the reward. Those who listen to Proverbs' teaching and follow God's ways will be richly blessed, with a 'garland to grace your head and a chain to adorn your neck' (1:9). On the other hand there is the warning and the punishment. Those who reject wisdom's advice will only follow a way that leads to death and the absence of God (1:19,28). While it may be unfashionable, it is helpful right at the start to hear the strong warning against living in a way that denies God – and has dire consequences. Despite these hard words, though, we must remember throughout these next seven weeks that what we do not see here is a 'Victorian schoolmaster God', with stick in hand, ready to punish at the slightest failure. The wisdom we will be learning about belongs to a loving Father God, yearning to pour out His heart to us and have a relationship with us (1:23).

This *Cover to Cover Bible Study* guide will take us through the whole of Proverbs. However, rather than reading the book through consecutively – which can become a bit tedious and repetitive – it will be broken down into some of its main themes (not every theme is covered in this guide and you may like to pick up on other themes as you go through the readings). Week 1 looks at chapters 1–9, which form a distinct introduction to the book as a whole, and Week 7 looks at chapters 30–31, which similarly form a neat conclusion (and we will also look at chapters 26 and 27, to 'mop up' those last two remaining chapters that have not been covered elsewhere). Weeks 2 to 6 then look at specific themes that come out continually when you read through the book: the power of speech, family relationships, the call to respond to people in need, money and work.

On a practical note, some of the Bible readings have verses in parenthesis after the chapter. This is because almost every chapter contains almost every theme and often the relevant proverbs for the week's theme are so dotted around the book that it becomes impossible to put down all the chapters that contain those proverbs. Instead, some of the most important chapters have been chosen and the verses that are specific to the week's theme then indicated in the brackets.

Can you remember the last time your church had a teaching series on Proverbs? Your answer is likely to be no because this book is not regularly taught in our churches. This is very much to our detriment because, for those prepared to do a little 'mining', it will become apparent that Proverbs contains a bounty of treasures waiting to be discovered. May you enjoy studying this wonderful book and gaining from the riches that are contained within it.

Note

1. If you want to find out more about the background questions of Proverbs, such as when it was written and to whom, see a commentary such as David Atkinson's, *The Message of Proverbs* (IVP, 1996).

WEEK 1

Proverbs 1-9: the Two Ways

Icebreaker

Apart from becoming a Christian (or getting married, if applicable), talk about the biggest choice you have had to make in your life so far. What were the options? What have been the results?

Bible Readings

- Proverbs 1–9 (you can omit chapters 5 and 7 if you like – see Leader's Notes)

Opening Our Eyes

The first nine chapters of Proverbs form a distinct section and are a series of poems rather than specific proverbs. They are in the form of two parents' words to their son as he reaches maturity. Their role, within the overall context of the book, is to set the framework within which the actual proverbs (in chapters 10 onwards) work.

The framework is of two ways that are set before the son, and before each one of us in our lives. On the one hand is the way of wisdom/righteousness. This is personified in the character of Lady Wisdom, in chapters 8 and 9 particularly. She makes a public invitation from the city gates (8:3) and calls all who are simple and foolish to listen to her and choose her instruction (8:10). On the other hand is the way of folly/evil. This is personified in the character of Lady Folly, in chapter 9. She also publicly invites those who are simple to choose her way (9:15–16). Both women call people into their respective homes, in which they have laid on a banquet. Wisdom's is sumptuous, with the choicest of foods (8:19; 9:5). To eat at her table leads to life and understanding (9:6). Folly, however, offers water that is 'stolen' and her guests have to eat 'in secret' (9:17). Those who sit down with her will receive only disaster and death (1:27; 9:18).

The idea of there being two ways set before us is a common theme in the Bible. It is most prominent in Moses' address to the people of Israel as they stand on the threshold of entering Canaan. He says to them, 'See, I set before you today life and prosperity, death and destruction' (Deut. 30:15). As the people go into the land that God has promised them and enter a new phase in their history, they have a choice. Will they 'choose life' and live under the blessing of God – loving Him, listening to His voice and holding fast to Him (vv.19–20), or will they be disobedient and follow other gods (v.17)? Jesus, too, talked about the wide road and the narrow road (Matt. 7:13–14). The narrow road is entered by a narrow gate that few go through, but – as above – leads to life, whereas the wide road is entered by a big gate that is easy to go through, but leads again to destruction. Similarly, Jesus contrasts the wise person who listens to Jesus' words and builds their life on them with the foolish person who does not listen to Jesus' words and finds their life crashing down around them (Matt. 7:24–27).

Jesus' words clearly echo the pictures given in Proverbs 1 to 9. Underlying these images is the understanding of God as a Creator God – creating the world and its people, giving that world structure and order and placing it within boundaries.[1] All that we see in Proverbs is to be seen within this understanding of our world and how it operates.

In this first week we also have the two ways laid out before us. We can see the benefits that following wisdom brings (eg 2:1–22). We can also see the consequences of ignoring Wisdom's call (eg 1:10–33). The question before us is which woman will we listen to? Will we ignore the words of this book and choose death, or will we follow its commandments and choose life?

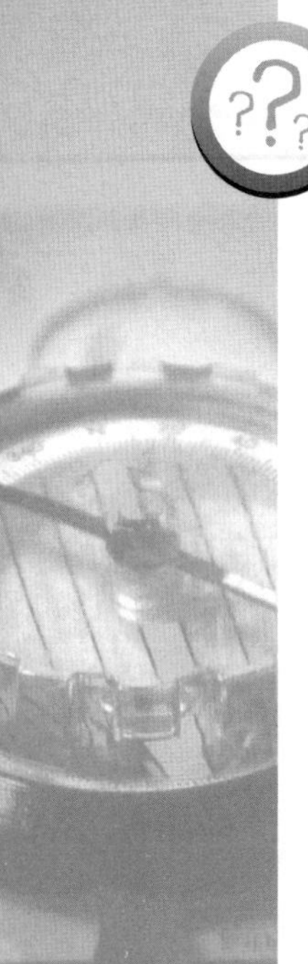

Discussion Starters

1. What is the 'fear of the Lord'? How is that the foundation for wisdom? Is it the basis for your life?

Respect/reverence for
Do what maker said.
Dwell in it with God at the centre.
Follow the designers way.

2. Make a list of all the things that are promised to us in 1:2–6 and 2:1–22 if we take on board the wisdom of the book of Proverbs.What do you think each one means? What might they look like in your life?

wisdom/discipline/understanding,
prudent/right, just, fair/knowledge/
discretion/learning/guidance
victory/shield/guards/protects/Love
getting more of God gets wisdom

3. Look at 1:10–33. What are the attractions of verses 11–14? What attitudes lie behind being lured by these things?

Gain of material things
greed, easy living

4. Proverbs 3 provides an excellent summary of a life lived in wisdom. Go through it point by point, discussing what each one means to you. How does Proverbs 3 counteract 1:10–33?

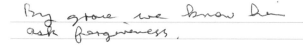

By grace we know Him
ask forgiveness.

5. Proverbs 4:23 is an interesting verse. What do you think this statement means? What do you need to do to ensure that your heart is guarded?

Will, Emotion, morality
Move God's 'world view'

6. Look at Proverbs 6:16–19. Can you think of examples where you have seen these things today? Put this list next to that of 4:23–27 to form a good summary of what we must not do.

7. In 8:1–3, Wisdom is described as raising her voice to all humanity. What other voices can distract us from hearing her call?

Folly, materialism, beauty of the world

8. Finish the session by taking 5 …10 …15 minutes to sit in silence and picture the scene in 9:1–6, reflecting particularly on verse 5. What does Wisdom say to you? Are there particular things that she gives you to eat or drink? (For more on this, see the Leader's Notes.)

Food + wine

Glorify God + ~~serve~~ enjoy Him forever

Personal Application

Proverbs 1–9 is a very dense section of the book, full of warnings, encouragements and advice. It can be easy to lose sight of what it is saying amidst all the detail. Take some time to think through what these first nine chapters are saying to you. Think of the benefits that wisdom brings and consider examples in your own life where you have learnt that following wisdom brings protection and blessing. Think also of the areas that we are warned against. Are there times when you have listened to Folly rather than to Wisdom and have reaped the consequences? Finally, look again at what we are promised if we follow Wisdom. As we start this Bible study, make a note of particular things you know you would like to gain in your life.

Seeing Jesus in the Scriptures

Proverbs 8:22–36 is a magnificent description of Wisdom personified and we see that she goes right to the very heart of who God is. The culmination is verse 31, which mirrors Genesis 1:31 and demonstrates God's attitude to His world – that He rejoices in it and loves it, with particular mention made of humanity. As Christians we cannot help but see the Person of Jesus reflected in these words. He, too, existed from the beginning (John 17:5), played an integral role in the creation of the world (Col. 1:15–17) and is in communion with God (John 1:1–3). Jesus is the true wisdom of God (1 Cor. 1:24): no wonder we are told, 'whoever finds me finds life' (v.35)!

Note

1. C. Bartholomew, *Reading Proverbs with Integrity* (Grove Books: Cambridge), p.10.

WEEK 2

Speech: the Power of the Tongue

Icebreaker

It has been said that you can tell the true character of a Christian by how they speak when they are behind the wheel of their car! What most frustrates you when you are driving and what is your speech like?

Bible Readings

- Proverbs 14, 15 and 16
- Romans 1:29–32 (optional)
- James 3:3–12 (optional)

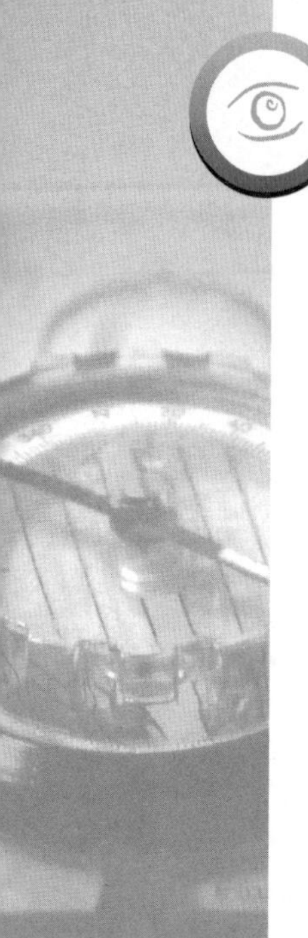

Opening Our Eyes

When I think about how we can use our tongue, two memories come to mind that have taught me valuable lessons about its power. The first is about being bullied in my final year at primary school. It was a verbal taunting started by a girl who had, up until that point, been my best friend. She turned lots of children in my class against me and I had a horrible last year. What happened that year affected me for years to come. It robbed me of my confidence and, even as an adult, if people were talking quietly together I would assume they were saying something bad about me.

The second is more recent and occurred within a circle of friends. Two people committed an offence and soon everyone was talking about it, giving their opinions and taking sides. No one had the sense either to break the circle of gossip and stop talking or to talk with someone from 'the other side' and bring about reconciliation. Long-standing friendships were lost and great damage was done.

Proverbs warns us against five very specific things with regards to speech. First, Proverbs warns against lying (eg 14:5; 15:4; 26:28). Secondly, it warns against using your tongue to make other people angry and stir up quarrels (eg 15:1; 17:19). Thirdly is the command not to speak too quickly, but to 'think before you speak', as we would say today (eg 15:2, 28). Fourthly, Proverbs warns us against speaking out of an ill-temper (eg 14:17; 15:18) and, finally, is the all-important command against gossiping (eg 17:4; 16:28).

Looking at these areas from a positive perspective, we see that the tongue can and should be used in ways that bring peace and blessing, always speaking the truth. To speak positive words can go against our cultural grain and it can be all too easy to find the negative. I am struck continually, in the work that I do with the Community Association where I live, how hard people find it to say something positive. If they can find something to complain about then they will! If there is silence then I know that people are pleased with what is happening … rarely will that actually be vocalized. I remember a friend of mine getting most frustrated with her husband because he refused to join in with her while she was complaining about someone. She said in exasperation, 'Oh he'll never say anything negative about anyone; he'll always find the positive.' What a wonderful thing to have said about you! It is true to say that we might never know what blessing we bring by a simple positive word spoken to someone at a particular moment.

So this week, we have the uncomfortable opportunity to take a long, hard look at how we use our speech. Do you use your tongue to do good or damage? Are you quick to react to an offence or do you know when to keep silent? Are you too easily drawn in to talking negatively about someone or are you brave enough to point out when people are gossiping? Does your tongue let you down when you are grumpy or can you control it? The way we use our tongues says a lot about our character. What does how you speak say about you?

11) 9, 13, 12
12, 6, 13, 17, 18, 19, 23, 22
14) 5, 17
15) 1, 2, 4, 28, 18
16) 28
17) 7, 4, 28

Discussion Starters

1. Read Romans 1:29–32 and James 3:3–12. What do they tell us about the importance of our speech?

Little effort can cause chaos.
Words reflect our inner most thoughts.

2. Why is it wrong to lie? What are some forms of lying in our modern world (eg spin, embellishment)?

Destroys trust. Commandment.

3. Is it ever right to lie? Have a look at Joshua 2:1–6 and Hebrews 11:31.

When we believe God's will
is being carried out.

4. Proverbs 15:28 tells us that 'the heart of the righteous weighs its answers, but the mouth of the wicked gushes evil'. What can you learn from that about some of the characteristics of a wise and godly person?

Think before you speak.

5. In what situations in your life do you come across gossip (eg work, friends, etc)?

6. Is talking about a person always gossip? How do you make the distinction?

No. Gossip destructive, poisonous. Talking positively, truth's not gossip.

7. Do you know people whose mouths 'run away with them' causing arguments, or who are unable to control their speech when they are angry? Why are they like that? What do you learn from them?

8. Has there been a time in your life when someone spoke just the right word to you? What was the result?

9. Do you face a particular situation in which you find it hard to speak positively? What might help you remember not to be so negative in your speech?

10. Who do you know who might benefit from a kindly word from you this week?

Personal Application

Proverbs has some beautiful words to say about how we use our tongues: 'a gentle answer turns away wrath'; 'the tongue that brings healing is a tree of life' (15:1, 4). There is so much good that we can do with our speech: healing wounds, quietening someone's bad temper, bringing peace. What power we have with such a small thing! This week, let us be more aware than usual of how we are talking and how our words affect those around us. Whether at home or at work or socialising with friends, we have opportunities either to harm someone or to bring them blessing. Let us make sure that our tongues are demonstrating wisdom and not foolishness.

Seeing Jesus in the Scripture

Jesus had lots to say about our speech and, again, reflects the teaching of Proverbs in His own words. He, too, taught that the way we use our tongues is a reflection of what is in our hearts (Matt. 12:33–37). If we are honest people, then we have no need of swearing by anything, for people can simply trust our word (Matt. 5:37). He advocated simplicity in our speech and taught that prayer should not be an occasion for showing off by babbling with lots of long words (Matt. 6:7). Along with Proverbs and James, Jesus recognised the great importance of our speech, saying people 'will have to give account on the day of judgment for every careless word they have spoken' (Matt. 12:36). Surely we need no further encouragement to watch our tongues!

Andrew Bourne

WEEK 3

Family Relationships: War and Peace

Icebreaker

What are your childhood memories of Christmas?

Bible Readings

- Proverbs 5 and 7
- Proverbs 13 (vv.1,22,24)
- Proverbs 17 (vv.1,6,17,21,25)
- Proverbs 19 (vv.7,13–14,18,26–27)
- Mark 3:31–35
- Luke 2:41–52

Opening Our Eyes

Families: do you love them or hate them? Perhaps you thrive in them and live closely to other family members, seeing them regularly and missing them when they are away. Or maybe you see families as things that have to be suffered. It doesn't cross your mind to prioritize maintaining contact with them and you view family gatherings with dread and dismay! Families are strange entities: made up of people who you might not be friends with in any other context, but to whom your sense of loyalty runs deep. With a potent mix of sometimes similar, sometimes different personalities and memories stretching back for years, it is no wonder that families can either be a source of love and security, or the cause of the most bitter disputes and hurts.

As we have seen already, Proverbs is written within the context of a father giving advice to his son, and so all the words we have been reading over these three weeks are set against a family background. It is no surprise, therefore, that family issues feature highly.

For Proverbs, families are hugely valuable and play an important role within society. There is much emphasis in Proverbs on the part that they play in forming a person's character and preparing them for their place in society more broadly. It is the immediate family that provides the foundational teaching place for life. What a child learns from their parents will stay with them for ever – whether good or bad. Where that teaching is good, Proverbs cannot state strongly enough how important it is to take note of it and learn from it: 'Listen … to your father's instruction and do not forsake your mother's teaching' (1:8). The foundation that good parenting can give a child is so fundamental that Proverbs describes it as being 'a garland to grace your head and a chain to adorn your neck' (1:9).

Proverbs thus describes both the responsibility (19:18) and the joy (15:20, and see 17:21) that comes from having children. It also talks about the children's responsibility to heed the instruction they are given (13:1) and the good things that come to a child from maintaining a good relationship with their parents (13:22). The reciprocal nature of a quality parent/child relationship is summed up perfectly in 17:6 where we are told that grandchildren are 'a crown to the aged' and that parents are 'the pride of their children'.

It is in the advice against adultery that we see the high value that Proverbs places on marriage. It provides us with one of the most beautiful descriptions of a happy, life-long monogamous relationship: that relationship is to 'be yours alone, never to be shared with strangers' and the young husband is encouraged always to *rejoice* in the wife of his youth, to be *satisfied* by her breasts and *captivated* by her love (5:17–19). Because of this, it is indeed true that 'houses and wealth are inherited from parents, but a prudent wife [or husband] is from the LORD' (19:14).

Families, then, provide the framework for us to grow and develop, to nurture and support one another. We are in family units to care for one another. Whatever our understanding is of family, Proverbs 17:1 is a good summary of our aim for them: that they are to be places where our focus is on peace rather than on material gain.

Discussion Starters

1. Families have been described as 'Covenants of Care'.[1] What experience have you had of this?

2. What are the pressures on parents today? Grandparents

Trying to have family life whilst both working

3. What are your thoughts on Proverbs 17:6?

Love our grandchildren

4. Proverbs does not mention any other type of family than two parents with their own children. How does that compare with what we see of families today? With these complex family situations, how can we apply Proverbs' words of wisdom?

With difficulty. Lots of families far removed from godly family.

5. It sounds nice, but do you agree with Proverbs 17:1?

Yes

6. Why does unfaithfulness occur in marriage?

Don't generalise
Grass on other side
No commitment / communication

7. If you are married, how can you protect your marriage from the attractions of unfaithfulness?

Don't be easily led

8. What role does the church have in applying what Proverbs says both to Christians and to wider society?

Encouraging family life

9. What do Mark 3:31–35 and Luke 2:41–52 teach us about the concept of family from a Christian perspective?

Wider than relations
God as our Father

Personal Application

How do you see yourself within the concept of family? You are no doubt somebody's daughter or son and you might also be a parent or a sibling, a spouse, a grandparent or all of these things together! Whatever 'position' you hold within your family/ies, Proverbs opens our eyes to the responsibilities and the privileges of being a part of that. We each have a responsibility of care to be looking after one another, helping others to walk closer to God's way of wisdom (whatever that may mean to individuals) and to be conducting ourselves in ways that honour and respect others. In turn, we should then reap the benefits of being part of a family that operates in that way. Use this week to think about what needs to happen for your family to be like that.

Seeing Jesus in the Scriptures

Hebrews 2:11 says that 'both the one who makes men holy and those who are made holy are of the same family. So Jesus is not ashamed to call them brothers'. We know that when we make a decision to follow Jesus, we become part of His family. Jesus and His followers are now our sisters and brothers and God is our Father. As we see from the Mark and Luke readings this week, this family supersedes our earthly family and now our primary responsibility is to them. This is where we find our true belonging and identity; this is the family that we should nurture and where we can be nurtured.

Note

1. David Atkinson, *The Message of Proverbs*, p.121.

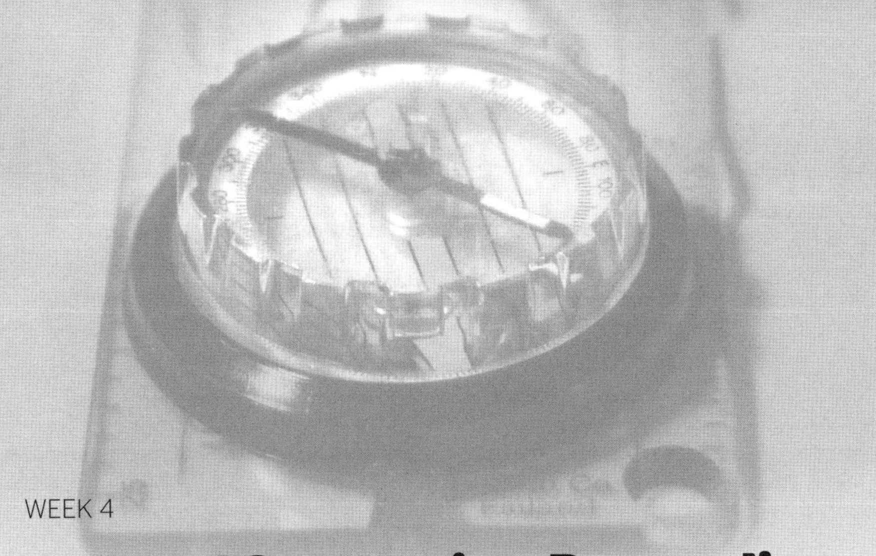

WEEK 4

Care and Compassion: Responding

Icebreaker

How well do you know your neighbours?

Bible Readings

- Proverbs 17:1–5
- Proverbs 21 (vv.3,10,13,15)
- Proverbs 22 (vv.2,9,16,22–28)
- Proverbs 25 (vv.8–11,16–19)
- Proverbs 28 (vv.3,5–6,8–11,22,27)
- Proverbs 29:1–14

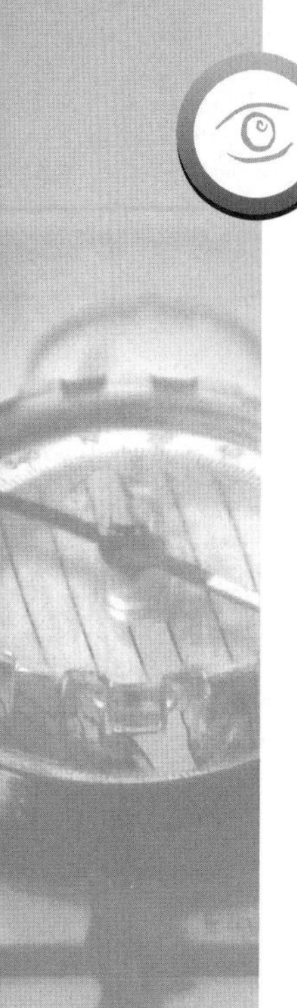

Opening Our Eyes

Last week we looked at how wisdom applies to our family situations and the challenge for us to be creating communities of care. We do not have to read through Proverbs for long, though, to realise that it is not just interested in our immediate relationships with those we know well, but is concerned with how we relate to *all* people, wherever they may live and however little we might know them.

Proverbs envisages a society where people know their neighbours well, and it is all too familiar with both the blessings but also the problems that can arise from living closely with others. Hence, it applies its wisdom, as practically as ever, to teaching us about good neighbourliness. There is a particular focus on this in chapter 25. Following on from what we saw in Week 2 on speech, this chapter encourages us not to lie about our neighbours (v.18), not to gossip about private matters (vv.9–10) and not to get into legal disputes (vv.7–8). Overall, Proverbs teaches us that we should live with our neighbours in peace and blessing (see also 3:29; 11:9; 24:28; 26:19).

Jesus teaches about the idea of neighbourliness in his story about the compassionate Samaritan in Luke 10 (vv.25–37). In answer to the question, 'who is my neighbour?', Jesus cleverly turns it round and, in effect, answers, '*You* are that neighbour, so go and do likewise' (v.37). We live in a very different cultural setting to the society that Proverbs was addressing, but as we look this week at the emphasis on caring for those in need, we can consider what it might mean for us to be that neighbour today. A part of what it means is being a good neighbour in our local community, in the literal sense that Proverbs would have envisaged for 'neighbourliness'.

Proverbs lays emphasis on justice and shows concern for those who are poor. Indeed, if we were to take out of Proverbs all the sayings that relate to justice and to the poor and needy, we would lose a lot of what the book has to say to us. Again, Proverbs is writing to a society where rich and poor probably rubbed shoulders a fair amount. We, however, are predominantly in the situation where the people in real poverty live in countries thousands of miles away from us. Thus, as people who belong to a worldwide Church and who believe that all people are made in God's image, it is clear that our 'neighbourliness' extends beyond our local area to include people all round the world.[1]

We live in a world of terrible inequalities, both between countries and within countries (for example, in the USA the top 10% of the population has six times the income of the lowest 20%). Despite encouraging advances in East and South Asia, the basic needs of many here are not being met. It is estimated that around 840 million people are chronically undernourished. In a world such as ours, Proverbs 21:13 speaks loudly: 'if a man shuts his ears to the cry of the poor, he too will cry out and not be answered'. Whether living next door or on the other side of the world, being wise is about responding with care and compassion to those who are in need.

Discussion Starters

1. Is Proverbs unique in the Bible in emphasising the theme of justice and care for the poor?

2. 'The justice of God is essentially concerned with a way of life for God's people which corresponds with the character of God's righteousness'.[2] Discuss this quote together (you could link it in with Proverbs 28:5 and 29:7).

3. Talk together about the area that you each live in. What needs are you aware of? If you are not aware of many, how can you find out?

4. How can you be a good neighbour – bringing blessing – to those in your area?

5. In what ways is the Church called to be a community that demonstrates care and compassion?

6. Share a story from a time in your own life when you have been in need and have been helped and supported by people around you.

7. Proverbs 13:23 perceptively states, 'a poor man's field may produce abundant food, but injustice sweeps it away'. What are the injustices in our world today that keep people in poverty?

8. We are all aware of the awful situations of poverty that so many millions face in our world today. Why do we not do more to help?

9. Proverbs 22:9 tells us that 'a generous man will himself be blessed, for he shares his food with the poor'. How practically can you demonstrate generosity to those who are poor?

Personal Application

There are so many ways in which we can be a good neighbour and demonstrate the good news of Jesus in our local community and wider world. There may be people in your street who have been beaten up by life and need you to look after their wounds. Perhaps there are broader community matters that you could get involved in through, for example, being on a residents' association. You can give financially to organisations that are working on the frontline to alleviate poverty. You can campaign. You can seek to live your life in a way that does as little damage as possible to God's world and the people who live in it (through, for example, buying fairly traded and organic goods). You have heard the words of wisdom from Proverbs on these matters. It is now up to you to do something about it!

Seeing Jesus in the Scriptures

When John's disciples went to Jesus to ask Him if He was the Messiah, He replied: 'Go back and report to John what you hear and see: The blind receive sight, the lame walk, those who have leprosy are cured, the deaf hear, the dead are raised, and the good news is preached to the poor' (Matt. 11:2–5). As the true Wisdom of God, it is no surprise that Jesus mirrors Proverbs' emphasis on justice and caring for those who are poor. He reached out to those who were excluded by society and showed compassion for social, spiritual and physical needs all together. Let us learn from His example!

Notes

1. To study this theme more fully see, Ruth Valerio, *Rivers of Justice: responding to God's call to righteousness today* (CWR Cover to Cover Bible Study, 2005).
2. David Atkinson, *The Message of Proverbs*, p.111.

WEEK 5

Money: Whom do we Trust?

Icebreaker

A Joseph Rowntree survey found that 95% of those questioned found it offensive to be asked about how they spent their money and whether the choices they were making could be improved upon. Would you put yourself in that 95%? Why?

Bible Readings

- Proverbs 13 (vv.4,7–8,11,18,21–22,25)
- Proverbs 18 (vv.10–11,23)
- Proverbs 23:1–8
- Proverbs 30:7–9
- Matthew 6:19–34

Opening Our Eyes

You may well be familiar with the song based on Proverbs 18:10 – 'Blessed be the name of the Lord'. You have probably had to endure singing it repeatedly in church meetings and doing the various actions that accompany it! It is a wonderful song that reminds us how safe we are with God. However, you have probably never sung the next verse: 'the wealth of the rich is their fortified city; they imagine it an unscalable wall' (v.11). These two verses highlight a very important contrast – putting your trust in God and putting your trust in money and material things.

This contrast is seen throughout the Bible. It emerges early in Israel's history after they have been rescued from Egypt and are in the desert, having to trust God literally to supply all their daily needs (and not trusting Him very well, as they grumble at every possible opportunity! See Exodus 15:22–27). It is seen further on in their history when they start to doubt God's ability to protect them from aggressive neighbours, reject His rule and choose instead to have a king, so that they might be 'like all the other nations' (1 Sam. 8:20).

Jesus states this contrast in the bluntest terms: 'you cannot serve both God and Money' (Matt. 6:24). This is a crucial choice for us to consider today in our societies that are so dominated by a love of money (the ultimate irony being the dollar bill which has 'in God we trust' emblazoned on it!). In what or whom do we put our trust? Proverbs 15:16 tells us, 'Better a little with the fear of the LORD than great wealth with turmoil,' while 16:16 says, 'How much better to get wisdom than gold, to choose understanding rather than silver!' In our heart of hearts, though, do we really believe that?

Trusting in God is the focus of Proverbs 22:17 to 23:18. It forms part of a little collection of proverbs called the 'Sayings of the Wise' (22:17–24:34), and the reason for them is given in 22:19 – 'So that your trust may be in the LORD'. Reading through these words gives an excellent summary of what we must do if *our* trust is to be in the Lord, and how our attitude towards money and material possessions goes hand in hand with much that we have studied in Proverbs. We should not only pay attention and listen to all that we have been reading in Proverbs, but should also be ready to put it into action (22:17–18). We should take care not to exploit the poor or allow rash and hot-tempered people to influence us or get ourselves into unwise debts (22:22–27). We should not take another person's property or means of livelihood (22:28). We should be wise in our attitude towards money, not craving it or the luxuries it brings (23:1–8). We should be wise in whom we give advice to and we should be careful to discipline our children.

It is important to notice that the foundation for all this is in our hearts (23:17). If we are consumed with zeal for God then, as Jesus said, our focus will not be on clothes and food, etc., but will be on God's kingdom and His justice and righteousness.

Discussion Starters

1. Go through this week's Bible readings. What are the main themes that come through regarding money?

2. In our predominantly affluent and comfortable lives, how does the contrast between trusting God and trusting money show itself?

3. What examples can you give from your own life where you have learnt that wealth is imagined to be 'an unscalable wall', but in reality the only 'strong tower' is the Lord?

4. If our lives are the best demonstration of our worship, what does the way you live your life say about who or what you worship? How does it differ from those around you who do not worship God?

5. Discuss the wisdom involved in Proverbs 30:8–9.

6. Some of the proverbs in this week's Bible readings would seem to support a 'prosperity theology', which teaches that financial prosperity is a sign of spiritual righteousness and blessing from God. Would you agree with that?

7. Picking up on our discussion from last week, what relevance does Proverbs 18:23 have for us?

8. In a similar manner way to how we ended Week 1, finish this session by meditating on Proverbs 18:10 (see Leader's Notes for more on this).

Personal Application

Jesus tells us, 'do not worry about your life, what you will eat or drink; or about your body, what you will wear. Is not life more important than food, and the body more important than clothes?' (Matt. 6:25). What is the focus for your life? It is good to consider where we put our energies – into the work of God's kingdom, or into making ourselves more financially secure and comfortable. We can often tell this by looking at what we spend most time thinking about! We live in a society that is obsessed with material security and it can be hard to break free of that. Will power alone will not work: we have to ask God to change our hearts by His Holy Spirit.

Seeing Jesus in the Scriptures

In John 10:10, Jesus says that He has come so that we 'may have life, and have it to the full'. Our culture tells us continually that happiness is about being healthy, wealthy, young and beautiful. It is profoundly individualistic and self-centred, and can be summed up by the L'Oreal advertising strap line 'because I'm worth it'. The gospel of Jesus tells us the opposite and Jesus promises that, in Him, we will find real, abundant life. True contentment, though, only comes about through a giving away of ourselves through service to others (Mark 8:35; Luke 22:24–27). It comes from being secure in the knowledge that money and possessions are not the focus of our lives: that honour belongs to Jesus.

WEEK 6

Work: 9 to 5 or 24/7?

Icebreaker

If your week could be described like a weather forecast, how would you describe it?

Bible Readings

- Proverbs 10
- Proverbs 11
- Proverbs 12
- Proverbs 20
- Proverbs 24

Opening Our Eyes

The alarm clock goes off and you leap out of bed with utter enthusiasm: hooray, it's another day at work! Does that describe you? How is work going for you as you read this? Perhaps you are bogged down in a pile of paperwork. Maybe you are excited by the challenges work presents. Do you live for your work, or simply for the weekend? Perhaps most importantly, does your life at work have anything to do with your life as a Christian?

There is some truth in the old cliché that, in days gone by, churches used to be concerned only with how their members behaved on Sunday. Work was of marginal significance – just something people had to do in order to earn money to live – and would never be addressed from the pulpit. What was *really* important was what part a person played in the church. It was often considered, therefore, that a person in 'full-time Christian ministry' was far more important than someone who worked outside of the church structure full time.

Thankfully this situation has been redressed and many churches now really encourage their members in the role they have in the workplace. Proverbs leads in this regard. As we have already seen, wisdom in Proverbs is not about a rarefied holiness that divorces the people of God from the rest of life, but it is about following God *in* that life and playing our part in it. Work, of course, is a part of that and Proverbs has much to teach us in this area.

Work in Proverbs is regarded as something that is good and that we should all be engaged in. There is a heavy emphasis on working hard and not being lazy. Of course, the society that Proverbs was speaking into was one where a person literally had to work in order to survive. Thus proverbs such as 'lazy hands make a man poor, but diligent hands bring wealth' (10:4) were very true indeed.

Honesty and integrity are two key concepts that Proverbs espouses regarding work. Linking in with wider biblical teaching (eg Lev. 19:35–36; Ezek. 45:9–10; Psa. 11:1; Amos 8:5). Proverbs is clear that all trade should be conducted fairly (eg 20:10; 11:1). Surely there is much for us to learn from here, both in a wider sense with our global trading rules, but also in our own personal conduct at work and the pressures that there can be on us to bend the rules to meet our targets successfully.

Proverbs 11, in particular, reflects on the selfless attitude that should pervade our approach to work. We are to be 'kind-hearted' (v.16), to 'give freely' (v.24), to be 'generous' (v.25) and to 'seek good' (v.27). Paul would seem to be taking his cue from Proverbs when he writes that a person should work so that they may 'have something to share with those in need' (Eph. 4:28). This ties in with a message that Proverbs is very keen for us to hear and follows on from what we saw last week: we must always remember that making money is not the most important thing in life. 'Wealth is worthless in the day of wrath, but righteousness delivers from death' (11:4). It is indeed more important to reap the sure rewards of righteousness than to earn 'deceptive wages' (11:18).

Discussion Starters

1. Think about your work (whether that be a profession of some sort, a caring role in the home, a voluntary job, etc.). Do you feel that it is something God has called you to do, or something that you undertake grudgingly, or are you somewhere in between?

2. What is the Bible's overall view on work (see Leader's Notes)? Discuss how that compares with approaches to work today.

3. What does it mean in your work situation for you to be honest and to have integrity?

4. How do you balance the necessity of earning money to meet financial responsibilities with the biblical injunction to be generous and share our money with those who are in need?

5. Do you have any encouraging stories to tell of incidents at work when you have known that God has been with you, giving you His wisdom?

6. In what ways does your church support the working lives of its members? Are there other things that it could do? How might you help in this regard?

7. Considering the emphasis now on encouraging people in their workplaces, do you think we have swung the pendulum too far and people are now reluctant to take on full-time roles within the church?

8. What have you learnt about wisdom over these last six weeks that you can apply into your work situation?

Personal Application

As we know, we spend the majority of our waking life at work and so the godly wisdom that we have been learning about in this guide is very applicable to each one of us in whatever we do under that category. Our working lives are so assumed, and such an integral part of who we are, that we do not often take the time to reflect on them. This week we have the opportunity to do just that, so take this chance to think through the work that you do. In the every day, humdrum routine, how do you incorporate God's values into what you do? Does your work life reflect your life as a Christian? There are many angles to consider, linking in with what we have seen already about our speech, our call to care and respond with compassion, and our approach towards material things. One thing you might like to do is pray for your work colleagues, that they may see something of God in you.

Seeing Jesus in the Scriptures

Jesus knew all about work. He was presumably brought up in the carpentry trade before He started His travelling ministry, and was surrounded by people of all sorts of professions: tax collectors, fishermen, housewives, farmers, soldiers … It is evident from His teaching and parables that He valued all that they did. His message was clear, though. The overall aim of our work should not be 'for food that spoils, but for food that endures to eternal life, which the Son of Man will give you' (John 6:27).

WEEK 7

Wisdom or Folly: Which Way Will You Go?

Icebreaker

What is the best bit of advice you have been given?

Bible Readings

- Proverbs 26 and 27
- Proverbs 30 and 31

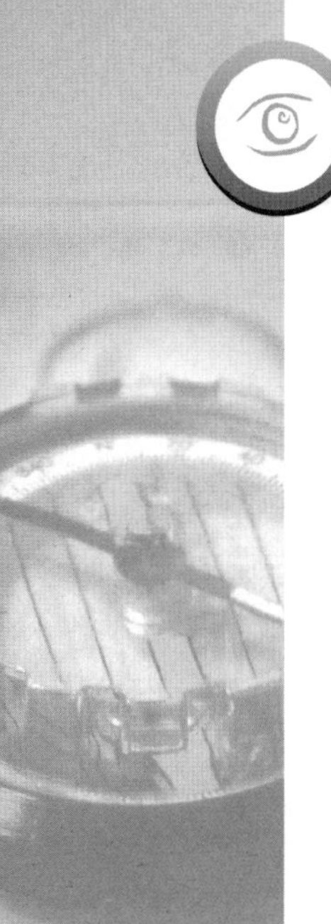

Opening Our Eyes

In many ways, this week's study brings us back to where we started from, thus providing a useful 'book-end' with Week 1. There we looked at the two ways that were set out before us: the way of wisdom or the way of folly, and we saw the invitation to choose one of those paths. Here, too, in this final set of readings we see the contrast between the wise person and the foolish.

Chapter 26 is a sustained attack on fools, sarcastic and disparaging in its tone. It says that the only thing fit for a fool is punishment (v.3), that a fool repeatedly does stupid things, 'as a dog returns to its vomit' (v.11), and that it is dangerous to ask a fool to say something wise (v.9). It is almost as if the book as a whole is saying, 'If you have not quite got the message, let me give it to you one last time …'. Choosing not to follow God and His ways is the most foolish thing we can do and it can only lead to disastrous consequences. As Proverbs 26:27 says, 'If a man digs a pit, he will fall into it; if a man rolls a stone, it will roll back on him.'

On the other hand is the 'wife of noble character' in Proverbs 31, who epitomizes true wisdom (the poem is acrostic in form: in the Hebrew, each line starts with the next letter of the alphabet, thus showing that she embodies wisdom 'from A to Z', so to speak). This is one remarkable woman! She is equally comfortable at home (v.27) or in society (v.31); with sharp business acumen (v.18) and compassion for the poor (v.20); faithful (v.12), wise (v.26) … the list goes on! She is a demonstration of how wisdom is not restricted to more 'religious' matters, but is concerned with every aspect of our lives. Proverbs 31:10–31 gives us a wonderful description of the results of choosing to live a life of wisdom.

Jesus, too, had a lot to say about fools and about those who were wise. Fools hear His words but do not put them into practice (Matt. 7:26). They do not prepare for the coming kingdom of God (Matt. 25:6). Fools are more concerned about religious trappings than the heart (Luke 11:40) and about present security rather than the future (Luke 12:20). In contrast, wise people – according to Jesus – live their lives in preparation for His return. Luke 12:35–48 is a graphic portrayal of the servants who are wise enough to keep watching and waiting for their master, however late He may be in returning, doing all the things that He has asked them to do.

The poem about the 'wife of noble character' is a fitting way to end this guide. It brings together what we have learnt about wisdom and helps us see how it applies to our own lives. It shows us, yet again, that wisdom is not a distant concept but is for people like us as we try to juggle work, family life, financial responsibilities, relationships, church commitments. The woman of Proverbs 31 has been described as 'a wonderful illustration … of Wisdom embodied, Wisdom lived out, Wisdom at home!'[1] May we, too, be such an illustration.

Discussion Starters

1. What advice for wise living do you find in chapters 26 and 27?

2. Read Luke 12:35–48. What does it mean to be always waiting for Jesus' return (v.36)? What would you like 'the master' to find you doing when He returns (v.43)?

3. What are some of the things you have learnt from nature in your life?

4. How can you allow the earth more space in your life to speak to you about the things of God?

5. What themes are emphasised by the advice to Lemuel from his mother? Is there any new advice for you to consider?

6. What can we learn from the advice to Lemuel for those of us who are in positions of leadership (in whatever sphere of life that leadership might be)?

7. Go through the description of the 'wife of noble character' and try to find modern-day equivalents for what is said of her. How does verse 30 contrast with attitudes towards women today?

8. Is there someone who has inspired you by being an illustration, him or herself, of 'wisdom lived out'?

9. In which area of your life do you think you are most in need of having the wisdom that we have been learning about in this guide?

Personal Application

The book of Proverbs is perhaps the book in the Bible that can be most easily applied to ourselves, and over the course of the last six weeks we have covered a wide array of topics relevant to each one of us in our everyday lives. Now we have one last opportunity to look at how we can apply the wisdom of Proverbs to ourselves. There is so much to consider in this week's four chapters. Maybe you know that you are a little too fond of alcohol and God is asking you to rein it in a bit (31:4–5). Perhaps you are still struggling to bring your tongue under control (26:22, 28), or need to accept some wise counsel from a good friend (27:9). Or maybe you are encouraged and inspired by the description of the woman in chapter 31 and want your life to mirror hers. Only you know which words have spoken to you from this week's readings. Whatever they are, commit them to God and ask Him to fill you with His Holy Spirit as you seek to follow His guiding.

Seeing Jesus in the Scriptures

Jesus, of course, is the ultimate embodiment of wisdom, of who the woman of Proverbs 31 is but a pale reflection. In the end, choosing God's way of wisdom means choosing to follow Jesus. We are only able to do that because He chose to die a horrendously painful death for us. Let us not forget what Jesus did for us so that we might be spurred on to live our lives for Him.

Note

1. David Atkinson, *The Message of Proverbs*, p.196.

Leader's Notes

Week 1: Proverbs 1-9

Icebreaker

This first icebreaker is designed to introduce the theme for this week's study and also enable people to begin getting to know one another. Do let the group take time to introduce themselves, if you do not already know each other. It is important that you help people to feel relaxed and comfortable and able to share with the group at the level that they feel happy with. As the weeks progress, so individuals will begin to talk more openly.

Bible Readings

While the readings for this week encompass chapters 1 to 9, chapters 5 and 7 will be looked at in more detail in Week 3 on Family Relationships. These can therefore be omitted if it is felt that the reading is too long.

Aim of Session

Proverbs 1 to 9 provides a brilliant introduction to the book as a whole and sets the scene well for understanding the actual proverbs themselves. The aim of this session is to get people thinking within the framework of the 'two ways' in life: the way of wisdom/righteousness and the way of folly/evil. As the Personal Application section draws out, this framework should be brought down to the personal level so that people begin seeing Proverbs not as a book of moral platitudes, but as containing guidance that speaks directly to them and their lives. It is incredible that, despite having been written thousands of years ago, its words are still so relevant to us today.

With that in mind, try to ensure that the discussion is always kept practical and relevant. Help people to avoid talking in clichés, which can often be a way of them avoiding an issue! For example, what does it actually *mean* for us to say that we should 'bind love and faithfulness around our necks' (3:3 – a possible answer to question 4)? What does it actually *mean* for us to say that wisdom will 'save us from the ways of wicked men' (2:12 – a possible answer to question 2)? Encourage people to give specific examples or illustrations for what they are saying.

Above all, this first week should get people excited as they read about the benefits of living the way of wisdom and begin to anticipate the difference that this Bible study could make to them.

The final question in the discussion starters is meditative and might cause a degree of anxiety for leaders who are not used to leading something like this. Depending on how the discussion has gone, it will be up to you to determine how long you spend on this. Ask people to close their eyes and get into a comfortable, but receptive, position. Read through Proverbs 9:1–6 again, slowly. Now talk people through imagining the scene envisaged here: they are walking down the street and hear Wisdom's invitation. They listen and decide to accept it. Imagine walking to Wisdom's magnificent house with its pillars, going in and finding the banqueting hall. Wisdom comes to greet you and leads you to her table. Let people take time picturing the table with all its wonderful food laid out on it. What do you see on the table? Invite people to enjoy seeing themselves sitting and eating. Now be quiet for a while and allow the Holy Spirit to move in people's lives. When you feel it is appropriate, bring the meditation to a close, perhaps by a simple prayer. If the group is happy to do so, you could take some time for people to share what God has been doing in/speaking to them.

Week 2: Speech

Icebreaker

This icebreaker makes a good talking point. It is about something that nearly everyone will be able to identify with and highlights a weakness that many people face – how you deal with the frustrations of driving when in the privacy of your car and no one else can hear you! The level of humour in this question will help to encourage people both to speak and to begin thinking about the uncomfortable question of how we talk.

Aim of Session

In church circles, when we look at anything to do with speech, we tend to focus on one area: swearing. This is, of course, very important; as we know from the third commandment in Exodus 20:7: 'You shall not misuse the name of the LORD your God'. The sad reality, though, is that while you may be in a church that has the Ten Commandments emblazoned above the altar, that same church may also be full of backbiting, gossip and negativity. Proverbs is brilliant in showing us that swearing is not the only issue when it comes to our speech (and indeed may not even be the most important issue).

Perhaps the main aim for this session is to help people to see that the way we talk is a reflection of our character; of what is going on in our hearts. Jesus' words, therefore, in the Seeing Jesus in the Scriptures section (Matt. 12:33–37) are particularly apt and worth bringing to people's attention. If we understand that the things we say are a reflection of our inner characters, then it will become clear that followers of Jesus should be concerned with every aspect of how they talk.

As well as broadening out discussions about speech beyond the area of blasphemy, try to encourage people to see just how important this whole topic for this week is. Romans 1 (you could also look at 1 Corinthians 6:9–10) is a good passage for discussion because it places these things (gossip, lying and so forth) on an equal footing with murder and sexual immorality: sins which, traditionally, Christians have given special prominence to. When we think of our lives, this can be a very challenging discussion indeed!

Finally, do be aware that this week's topic can be quite emotive. One reason for this is that it is an area that we fall down in so often. Do not let people fob the discussion off by making light of the topic. The group joker can sometimes be the one who is most trying to avoid the issue! Another reason for the sensitivity of this topic is that our speech is a reflection of our character. Once we have understood this, it can raise some disturbing questions that some people might be reluctant to face. So, be aware of what responses might be triggered in the group, but don't be afraid to make it personal and pin people down either!

Week 3: Family Relationships

Icebreaker

In the UK, Christmas is the climax of family life and comes with a whole bundle of expectations. It can either be a wonderful time – the highlight of the year that everyone enjoys – or a complete disaster, with family feuds and upsets! Christmas can often be a good reflection of the quality of a family. Childhood memories can be very revealing and can throw up some interesting surprises, yet within the safe context of talking about something that we all understand. Do be aware, though, that this question could be painful for some and so let people pass on the question if they wish. Be careful, too, that this icebreaker does not turn into a group therapy session or become dominated by one person's family difficulties.

Aim of Session

Yet again we see how wonderfully practical the book of Proverbs is as it turns its attention to something that we all deal with every day. However, as a leader you need to be aware that the issue of family can be a very emotive one that brings up deep issues within a person's life – sometimes things that they may not have talked about before. You need to exercise wisdom yourself in deciding how to tackle this week's questions.

The discussion can be kept at quite a superficial level, looking at family issues in our society today and keeping things quite impersonal. If you are able, though, and you feel the group knows each other well enough to be more open, you can take the discussion to a deeper level, asking people to be more personal in their answers. Do be aware of any issues that might arise in people as they talk and do not be afraid to stop the discussion for prayer if you think that would be appropriate.

When dealing with this subject of family, it is important to be inclusive and remember that not everyone in the group will be part of a classic nuclear family – two parents in a life-long marriage and their children. 'Family' means so many different things today, and singleness is much more common in our society than at the time Proverbs was written as many people are either staying single for longer or becoming single again after a marriage break-up. However, whatever situation individuals are in, everyone is part of a family somehow and so the majority of the questions will still be relevant to them.

Perhaps the most sensitive question revolves around Proverbs 5 and the subject of unfaithfulness. This issue may have touched more people in your group than you realize. There may be some who have actually experienced it for themselves and are now in the process of rebuilding their lives, or who are supporting a friend through something similar. There may be some who have been married for a long while and now find themselves, with children leaving home, wondering if they still have a relationship with their husband or wife, tempted towards someone else who seems to offer them something more. Maybe some are single and are drawn towards an attractive married man at work or in church, or there may be some in your group who are newly wed and could not imagine how they could possibly find someone else attractive or that their relationship might ever cause their partner to stray.

Be aware that people's lives (often their 'thought lives') can be quite different to how they appear on the outside. It could be helpful at some stage to let your group know of people they can talk to/places they can go if any of this is raising issues that they would like to talk about outside of the group.

Week 4: Care and Compassion

Icebreaker

When I was growing up, everyone in our road knew each other. Front doors were left open, the milk money could be put out the night before and the children were in and out of each other's houses. This is a stark contrast to how many of us live today, where we hardly know our neighbours' names, let alone feel free to pop in to their homes. Looking at this contrast is a good way of introducing our theme for this week.

Aim of Session

It can be easy to characterise wisdom as being primarily concerned with matters of individual purity and it can come as a surprise to read such a strong emphasis in Proverbs on caring for neighbours, having compassion on those who are in need, and seeking justice for people struggling with poverty. The aim of this session, therefore, is to help people see that issues of justice and poverty are right at the heart of Proverbs' message.

Question 1 aims to show that these issues are foundational to the whole message of the Bible. To answer question 1 more fully, you could look at the story of Cain and Abel (especially Gen. 4:9); the declaration to Noah (Gen. 9:5,6); the many descriptions of how Israel was to conduct herself (eg Lev. 25:8ff.; Deut. 24:10–22; Isa. 58); the example of Jesus (eg Matt. 25:31–46; Luke 4:16–21) and the picture of the Early Church (eg Acts 2:42–47; James 1:26–2:26).

Questions 3 and 4 ask you to look more closely at the area you live in and talk about the needs that are present and what you can do to respond. This may be a challenge because the reality is that we are often not very connected into where we actually live (we just have our house there: we work, play and worship elsewhere). A group of churches in my area spent a week doing things for people on the estate where I live – clearing gardens, washing cars, etc. It was a real eye-opener into the various situations that people were living in and the level of need that was there. Do encourage people to find out what facilities there are in their local area that will help them both to become more aware of what the needs are and then also to respond to them (for example, a residents' association, community volunteering group and so on).

Finally, regarding Question 7, I am always amazed at how contemporary Proverbs 13:23 sounds. Time and again you hear of people working hard to pull themselves out of poverty, but prevented from doing so because of the unjust structures that are around them. The way our global trading system works is one reason for the increasing inequality that our world is facing. The rules for international trade are governed by the commercial and financial interests of the economically richer countries and so are shaped to their advantage. There is no doubt that increasing exports to richer countries is a key way in which a poorer country can lift itself out of poverty and yet the poorest countries' share of world trade is only 0.4%. Another reason is the massive burden of debt that countries have accumulated. Rich countries get more and more money from the poor countries, which are then increasingly impoverished and unable to spend adequate money on basic needs such as healthcare and education. These are complicated questions and you might like to prepare yourself by getting hold of some information from the Make Poverty History campaign. See www.MAKEPOVERTYHISTORY.org.

Week 5: Money

Icebreaker

Talking about money on a personal level is taboo – in our churches as much as in society. We might feel free to share the intricacies of our 'spiritual life', but feel defensive when asked to share about how much we earn and how we spend it. And yet, how we use our money is as much a part of what it means to follow Jesus as how much we pray or fast (Matt. 6:1–24). Hence, if we want our spiritual lives to be healthy, then we have to be open about our finances and willing to be corrected. This icebreaker is good because it starts to open this whole area up for discussion.

Aim of Session

Again in this session, we see how godly wisdom is not only concerned with matters of 'inner purity', but directly addresses the practical realities of everyday life. Our attitude towards money, and how we use it, is of immense importance to Proverbs, and should be to each one of us who desires to live their life for God.

As always, we must take care in this session that we are being inclusive in our discussion. There may well be a variety of different financial situations in your group, from those who are financially comfortable to those for whom money is a daily struggle. It is likely that the majority will have a satisfactory income, but still find it tough to meet the demands of a mortgage, consumer lifestyle and expensive children. One person's comments might demonstrate a level of financial security that could trigger frustration and jealousy in someone else. So do be aware of the dynamics within the group and, as always, help people to be gracious and sensitive towards others.

As Question 1 indicates, Proverbs' teaching on money covers many themes, beyond that of trust that has been the focus of this session. You may well want to look at some of these other themes. A plethora of practical issues might arise, including lending, borrowing and debt, and individuals in the group might have specific questions as to how they can bring their finances under control. You cannot cover every financial topic in your discussion, but a good organisation to point people towards if they want practical advice is Credit Action (www.creditaction.com). Question 6 might raise some interesting views and issues! Some of the proverbs, taken individually and read apart from their wider contexts, can indeed be used to support both prosperity theology and the materialism of our culture. However, to read them in isolation is to misread them and there are many other proverbs that demonstrate a more multifaceted understanding of how God works. So, for example, there are proverbs that readily recognize that often there is *not* a cause-and-effect principle operating that sees the righteous rewarded with wealth and the evil cast into poverty (eg 15:16–17; 16:16). Put in its context of the wider wisdom material, which gives great space for the reality of suffering, pain and uncertainty, to use Proverbs to support prosperity teaching is to misuse it.

Question 8 again allows for a period of quiet meditation at the end of your discussion. Follow the beginning of the advice for Week 1 and then read out Proverbs 18:10 slowly a couple of times. Ask people to repeat it to themselves a few times (having Bibles open will help), like cows chewing the cud and getting all the goodness out. After a period of silence, allowing God to speak, bring the meditation to a close.

Week 6: Work

Icebreaker

This icebreaker is a good way of getting people to talk about themselves and their everyday lives. Depending on when in the week you are meeting, you can use this icebreaker as a description of how the week has been so far, or as a prediction of what people are expecting (or as a bit of both). If the group does not know each other that well, you could also ask people to give a brief description of the work they do before giving their 'weather forecast'.

Bible Readings
You will notice this week that specific verses have not been given in parenthesis after the main chapter reference. This is because, while some verses make explicit reference to the subject of work (eg Prov. 10:4), there are many other verses that are still very relevant (eg 10:2). This week in particular it is clear that so much of what we have already looked at in this guide is relevant also to the subject of work. The nature of our speech, having compassion for the poor, seeking justice and our attitude towards money are all appropriate things to consider when looking at our work.

Aim of Session
The main aim for this session is, of course, to look at how we can apply what we have been learning about godly wisdom to our working lives, which form such a vital part of our daily lives. As mentioned in the Personal Application section, it can be quite rare in our churches to get a specific opportunity to reflect on our work situation and how we bring God's values into it, and so this week should be refreshing (and hopefully slightly challenging!) to your group.

As has been stressed so often before, remember to be inclusive towards those who are not in straightforward '9 to 5' jobs. You may have stay-at-home parents in your group or people who are unemployed; someone with a long-term illness that prevents them from being in paid employment or those who are retired or caring for elderly relatives. Many different situations may be represented in your group, so allow individuals the opportunity both to say how they feel this word 'work' relates to them and also how they see themselves as fitting into your discussions.

Question 2 asks for a broader look at the Bible's view on work and it might be helpful to set that out briefly here. Proverbs' teaching is set within the context of a wider biblical understanding that work is good, something that is given to us from God. It is based on the idea that God Himself is a worker. Genesis 2:2, Colossians 1:16–17, Deuteronomy 11:1–7 and John 4:34 all give us an idea of some of the many things He does, and Psalm 111:2 tells us that all His works are 'great'. God has created us also to be workers and Ecclesiastes 3:13 and 5:18–19 describe work as a gift from God, an activity of great dignity and significance. Work is thus an important aspect of our self-fulfilment as people, rather than something to be avoided at all costs! As a part of this, God has created us to be co-workers with Him. 1 Corinthians 3:5–9, Genesis 2:8–15 and Psalm 8 paint a wonderful picture of the model of partnership that God envisages having with us. It can be helpful to point out as well that the Bible does not see work through rose-tinted spectacles and is quite ready to admit that work, since the Fall, can be full of drudgery and boredom (Gen. 3:19; Eccl. 2:19–23)![1]

Week 7: Wisdom or Folly

Icebreaker

In this, our final session, we are not focusing on one particular issue, so the icebreaker is designed more to get people chatting and thinking about the overall theme of wisdom. Hopefully you might glean some interesting comments from your group that will lead to further insight into people's lives.

Aim of Session

As stated in the Opening Our Eyes section, this final week mirrors Week 1 as we look at the general theme of wisdom and the difference between those who are wise and those who are foolish. It gives people one last opportunity to see how this unique book in biblical literature – written thousands of years ago – is still relevant to us now, and to discuss how its wisdom can be applied to our lives.

A word about a couple of the questions might be helpful. Questions 3 and 4 pick up on Proverbs 30, which does not get mentioned in the Opening Our Eyes section. It is an interesting chapter, different to the many others we have looked at so far, that shows us one arena in which we can learn about the difference between wisdom and folly. We have seen previously that the people we spend our time with have a lot to teach us, both negatively and positively, and how we are opened up to the wisdom of the earth as we see here how much we humans have to learn from the world of nature. Proverbs 30:2–4 is an awesome description of the difference between humanity and God, reminiscent of Job 28:12–28. It shows the power and immensity of God as He is able simply to 'gather up the wind in the hollow of his hands' and 'wrap up the waters in his cloak' (v.4). Creation bears God's fingerprints and has much to teach us of God's character.

It might be helpful here to remind people how much Jesus drew on the natural world in His teaching, using everyday pictures from the world around Him that would have been very familiar to those listening (eg mustard seeds, yeast and fig trees: Luke 13:18–20; Matt. 21:18–22). Perhaps best known is the lesson He draws out from the birds of the air and the flowers and grass in the field, teaching us that we should not worry about how we will eat or clothe ourselves because God will look after us. Our main focus instead should be on God's kingdom and on His justice and righteousness (Matt. 6:25–34). You can link this in with Proverbs 30:7–9.

In the light of the woman of Proverbs 31, question 7 looks at how women are viewed today. Our society – and hence we – can have a confused vision of what women should be like. On the one hand, women are told that they should be 'true to themselves' and that size and looks do not matter. On the other hand, magazines focus on women who are physically beautiful, with big breasts and no cellulite on their bottoms, and TV shows concentrate on helping women wear the right (expensive) clothes and look 'ten years younger'. Some aspects of our culture encourage women to find fulfilment in staying at home, looking after and nurturing the next generation, while others want the next generation to be in childcare, so women can find fulfilment in their careers. These throw up many social issues that are important to us all, but are not always given space for discussion in our church settings. To do so here might be helpful.

Note

1. For more on a biblical view of work see Session 6 on work in J. Odgers, *Simplicity, Love and Justice* (Alpha International, 2004) and the chapter 'J is for Jobs' in R. Valerio, *L is for Lifestyle: Christian living that doesn't cost the earth* (IVP, 2004).

National Distributors

UK: (and countries not listed below)

CWR, Waverley Abbey House, Waverley Lane, Farnham, Surrey GU9 8EP.
Tel: (01252) 784700 Outside UK (44) 1252 784700 Email: mail@cwr.org.uk

AUSTRALIA: KI Entertainment, Unit 21 317-321 Woodpark Road, Smithfield, New South Wales 2164.
Tel: 1 800 850 777 Fax: 02 9604 3699 Email: sales@kientertainment.com.au

CANADA: David C Cook Distribution Canada, PO Box 98, 55 Woodslee Avenue, Paris, Ontario N3L 3E5.
Tel: 1800 263 2664 Email: sandi.swanson@davidccook.ca

GHANA: Challenge Enterprises of Ghana, PO Box 5723, Accra.
Tel: (021) 222437/223249 Fax: (021) 226227 Email: ceg@africaonline.com.gh

HONG KONG: Cross Communications Ltd, 1/F, 562A Nathan Road, Kowloon.
Tel: 2780 1188 Fax: 2770 6229 Email: cross@crosshk.com

INDIA: Crystal Communications, 10-3-18/4/1, East Marredpalli, Secunderabad – 500026, Andhra Pradesh. Tel/Fax: (040) 27737145 Email: crystal_edwj@rediffmail.com

KENYA: Keswick Books and Gifts Ltd, PO Box 10242-00400, Nairobi.
Tel: (020) 2226047/312639 Email: sales.keswick@africaonline.co.ke

MALAYSIA: Canaanland, No. 25 Jalan PJU 1A/41B, NZX Commercial Centre, Ara Jaya, 47301 Petaling Jaya, Selangor. Tel: (03) 7885 0540/1/2 Fax: (03) 7885 0545 Email: info@canaanland.com.my

Salvation Publishing & Distribution Sdn Bhd, 23 Jalan SS 2/64, 47300 Petaling Jaya, Selangor.
Tel: (03) 78766411/78766797 Fax: (03) 78757066/78756360 Email: info@salvationbookcentre.com

NEW ZEALAND: KI Entertainment, Unit 21 317-321 Woodpark Road, Smithfield, New South Wales 2164, Australia. Tel: 0 800 850 777 Fax: +612 9604 3699 Email: sales@kientertainment.com.au

NIGERIA: FBFM, Helen Baugh House, 96 St Finbarr's College Road, Akoka, Lagos.
Tel: (01) 7747429/4700218/825775/827264 Email: fbfm_1@yahoo.com

PHILIPPINES: OMF Literature Inc, 776 Boni Avenue, Mandaluyong City.
Tel: (02) 531 2183 Fax: (02) 531 1960 Email: gloadlaon@omflit.com

SINGAPORE: Alby Commercial Enterprises Pte Ltd, 95 Kallang Avenue #04-00, AIS Industrial Building, 339420. Tel: (65) 629 27238 Fax: (65) 629 27235 Email: marketing@alby.com.sg

SOUTH AFRICA: Struik Christian Media, 1st Floor, Wembley Square II, Solan Street, Gardens, Cape Town 8001. Tel: +27 (0) 23 460 5400 Fax: +27 (0) 21 461 7662 Email: info@struikchristianmedia.co.za

SRI LANKA: Christombu Publications (Pvt) Ltd, Bartleet House, 65 Braybrooke Place, Colombo 2.
Tel: (9411) 2421073/2447665 Email: christombupublications@gmail.com

USA: David C Cook Distribution Canada, PO Box 98, 55 Woodslee Avenue, Paris, Ontario N3L 3E5, Canada. Tel: 1800 263 2664 Email: sandi.swanson@davidccook.ca

CWR is a Registered Charity - Number 294387
CWR is a Limited Company registered in England - Registration Number 1990308

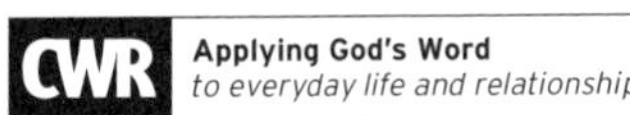

CWR
Applying God's Word
to everyday life and relationships

CWR, Waverley Abbey House,
Waverley Lane, Farnham,
Surrey GU9 8EP, UK

Telephone: **+44 (0)1252 784700**
Email: **info@cwr.org.uk**
Website: **www.cwr.org.uk**

Registered Charity No 294387
Company Registration No 1990308

Dramatic new resource

Judges 9-21 - Learning to live God's way

by Phin Hall

Having learned about the nature and nurture of faith in the first eight chapters of Judges, this study guide seeks to grow our faith in the certainty that God's ways are best.

72-page booklet, 148x210mm

ISBN: 978-1-85345-910-8

The bestselling *Cover to Cover* Bible Study Series

1 Corinthians
Growing a Spirit-filled church
ISBN: 978-1-85345-374-8

2 Corinthians
Restoring harmony
ISBN: 978-1-85345-551-3

1 Timothy
Healthy churches - effective Christians
ISBN: 978-1-85345-291-8

23rd Psalm
The Lord is my shepherd
ISBN: 978-1-85345-449-3

2 Timothy and Titus
Vital Christianity
ISBN: 978-1-85345-338-0

Acts 1-12
Church on the move
ISBN: 978-1-85345-574-2

Acts 13-28
To the ends of the earth
ISBN: 978-1-85345-592-6

Barnabas
Son of encouragement
ISBN: 978-1-85345-911-5

Ecclesiastes
Hard questions and spiritual answers
ISBN: 978-1-85345-371-7

Elijah
A man and his God
ISBN: 978-1-85345-575-9

Ephesians
Claiming your inheritance
ISBN: 978-1-85345-229-1

Esther
For such a time as this
ISBN: 978-1-85345-511-7

Fruit of the Spirit
Growing more like Jesus
ISBN: 978-1-85345-375-5

Galatians
Freedom in Christ
ISBN: 978-1-85345-648-0

Genesis 1-11
Foundations of reality
ISBN: 978-1-85345-404-2

God's Rescue Plan
Finding God's fingerprints on human history
ISBN: 978-1-85345-294-9

Great Prayers of the Bible
Applying them to our lives today
ISBN: 978-1-85345-253-6

Hebrews
Jesus - simply the best
ISBN: 978-1-85345-337-3

Hosea
The love that never fails
ISBN: 978-1-85345-290-1

Isaiah 1-39
Prophet to the nations
ISBN: 978-1-85345-510-0

Isaiah 40-66
Prophet of restoration
ISBN: 978-1-85345-550-6

James
Faith in action
ISBN: 978-1-85345-293-2

Jeremiah
The passionate prophet
ISBN: 978-1-85345-372-4

John's Gospel
Exploring the seven miraculous signs
ISBN: 978-1-85345-295-6

Joseph
The power of forgiveness and reconciliation
ISBN: 978-1-85345-252-9

Judges 1-8
The spiral of faith
ISBN: 978-1-85345-681-7

Judges 9-21
Learning to live God's way
ISBN: 978-1-85345-910-8

Mark
Life as it is meant to be lived
ISBN: 978-1-85345-233-8

Moses
Face to face with God
ISBN: 978-1-85345-336-6

Names of God
Exploring the depths of God's character
ISBN: 978-1-85345-680-0

Nehemiah
Principles for life
ISBN: 978-1-85345-335-9

Parables
Communicating God on earth
ISBN: 978-1-85345-340-3

Philemon
From slavery to freedom
ISBN: 978-1-85345-453-0

Philippians
Living for the sake of the gospel
ISBN: 978-1-85345-421-9

Prayers of Jesus
Hearing His heartbeat
ISBN: 978-1-85345-647-3

Proverbs
Living a life of wisdom
ISBN: 978-1-85345-373-1

Revelation 1-3
Christ's call to the Church
ISBN: 978-1-85345-461-5

Revelation 4-22
The Lamb wins! Christ's final victory
ISBN: 978-1-85345-411-0

Rivers of Justice
Responding to God's call to righteousness today
ISBN: 978-1-85345-339-7

Ruth
Loving kindness in action
ISBN: 978-1-85345-231-4

The Covenants
God's promises and their relevance today
ISBN: 978-1-85345-255-0

The Divine Blueprint
God's extraordinary power in ordinary lives
ISBN: 978-1-85345-292-5

The Holy Spirit
Understanding and experiencing Him
ISBN: 978-1-85345-254-3

The Image of God
His attributes and character
ISBN: 978-1-85345-228-4

The Kingdom
Studies from Matthew's Gospel
ISBN: 978-1-85345-251-2

The Letter to the Colossians
In Christ alone
ISBN: 978-1-85345-405-9

The Letter to the Romans
Good news for everyone
ISBN: 978-1-85345-250-5

The Lord's Prayer
Praying Jesus' way
ISBN: 978-1-85345-460-8

The Prodigal Son
Amazing grace
ISBN: 978-1-85345-412-7

The Second Coming
Living in the light of Jesus' return
ISBN: 978-1-85345-422-6

The Sermon on the Mount
Life within the new covenant
ISBN: 978-1-85345-370-0

The Tabernacle
Entering into God's presence
ISBN: 978-1-85345-230-7

The Ten Commandments
Living God's Way
ISBN: 978-1-85345-593-3

The Uniqueness of our Faith
What makes Christianity distinctive?
ISBN: 978-1-85345-232-1

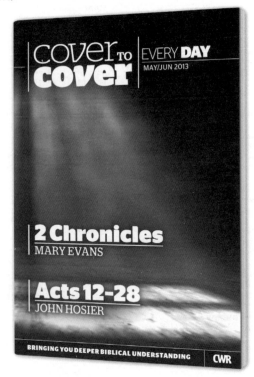

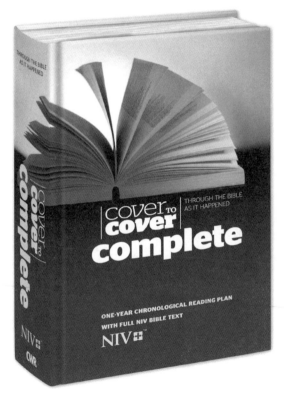